HANDS-ON SCIENCE PROJECTS

EARTH

FIND OUT ABOUT THE PLANET, EARTHQUAKES, VOLCANOES AND WEATHER WITH 50 GREAT EXPERIMENTS AND PROJECTS

CONSULTING EDITOR:
CHRIS OXLADE

southwater

This edition is published by Southwater,
an imprint of Anness Publishing Ltd,
Hermes House, 88–89 Blackfriars Road, London SE1 8HA;
tel. 020 7401 2077; fax 020 7633 9499

www.southwaterbooks.com; www.annesspublishing.com

If you like the images in this book and would like
to investigate using them for publishing, promotions
or advertising, please visit our website
www.practicalpictures.com for more information.

UK agent: The Manning Partnership Ltd;
tel. 01225 478444; fax 01225 478440;
sales@manning-partnership.co.uk
UK distributor: Grantham Book Services Ltd;
tel. 01476 541080; fax 01476 541061;
orders@gbs.tbs-ltd.co.uk
North American agent/distributor: National Book Network;
tel. 301 459 3366; fax 301 429 5746; www.nbnbooks.com
Australian agent/distributor: Pan Macmillan Australia;
tel. 1300 135 113; fax 1300 135 103;
customer.service@macmillan.com.au
New Zealand agent/distributor: David Bateman Ltd;
tel. (09) 415 7664; fax (09) 415 8892

Publisher: Joanna Lorenz
Managing Editor: Linda Fraser
Project Editor: Jennifer Schofield
Production Controller: Claire Rae
Consultant: Chris Oxlade
Contributing Authors: John Farndon, Jen Green,
Robin Kerrod, Chris Oxlade, Steve Parker, Rodney Walshaw
Designer: Axis Design Editions Ltd
Photographers: Paul Bricknell, John Freeman, Don Last,
Robert Pickett, Tim Ridley
Illustrators: Cy Baker/Wildlife Art, Stephen Bennington, Peter Bull Art Studio,
Stuart Carter, Simon Gurr, Richard Hawke, Nick Hawken, Michael Lamb,
Alan Male/Linden Artists, Guy Smith, Clive Spong, Stephen Sweet/Simon Girling
and Associates, Alisa Tingley, John Whetton
Stylists: Ken Campbell, Jane Coney, Marion Elliot, Tim Grabham, Thomasina Smith,
Isolde Sommerfeldt, Melanie Williams

ETHICAL TRADING POLICY

Because of our ongoing ecological investment programme, you, as our customer, can have
the pleasure and reassurance of knowing that a tree is being cultivated on your behalf to
naturally replace the materials used to make the book you are holding. For further
information about this scheme, go to www.annesspublishing.com/trees

Previously published as *Hands-On Science: Earth*

PUBLISHER'S NOTE

Although the advice and information in this book are believed to be accurate and true at the time
of going to press, neither the authors nor the publisher can accept any legal responsibility or
liability for any errors or omissions that may be made. The publishers have made every effort to
ensure that all instructions contained within this book are accurate and safe, and cannot accept
liability for any resulting injury, damage or loss to persons or property however they may arise.

Contents

Our Restless Earth

Earthquakes and volcanoes are a reminder that the Earth's surface is constantly and dramatically changing. Fossils reveal how many kinds of plants and animals that were once alive have now disappeared. Scientists realize that it is part of the Earth's nature to undergo violent changes caused by natural processes that act over billions of years. In the following pages, you can discover how some of these natural processes, such as wind erosion, rivers and mountain formation, affect the Earth.

Spinning planet

North Pole

beams of sunlight

Equator

South Pole

The Earth is like a giant ball spinning in the darkness of Space. The only light falling on it is the light of the Sun glowing 150 million kilometres away. The Earth turns once a day, and it orbits the Sun once a year. The experiments on these pages investigate both ways of moving, and explain why night and day and the seasons occur. The ball represents the Earth and the torch the Sun. In the final project, you can make a simple thermometer using water to record changes in temperature from night to day and from season to season.

▲ Variable sunlight

The Sun's light does not fall evenly over the Earth because our planet is round. Imagine three identical beams of sunlight falling on the Earth. One falls on the Equator and the others on the North and South Poles. The beam falling on the Equator covers a much smaller area, so its energy is more concentrated and the temperature is higher.

YOU WILL NEED

Night and day: felt-tipped pen, plastic ball, piece of thin string, non-hardening modelling material, torch.

The seasons: felt-tipped pen, plastic ball, bowl just big enough for the ball to sit on, torch, books or a box to set the torch on.

Make a thermometer: water, bottle, food colouring, clear straw, reusable adhesive, card, scissors, felt-tipped pen.

Night and day

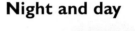

Draw or stick a shape on the ball to represent your country. Stick the string to the ball with modelling material. Tie the string to a rail, such as a towel rail, so that the ball hangs freely.

2 Shine the torch on the ball. If the country you live in is on the half of the ball in shadow on the far side, then it is night because it is facing away from the Sun.

3 Your home country may be on the half of the ball lit by the torch instead. If so, it must be daytime here because it is facing the Sun. Keep the torch level, aimed at the middle.

4 Turn the ball from left to right. As you turn the ball, your country will move from the light half to the dark half. You can see how the Sun comes up and goes down as the Earth turns.

The seasons

1 Use the felt-tipped pen to draw a line around the middle of the ball. This represents the Equator. Sit the ball on top of the bowl so that the Equator line is sloping gently.

2 Put the torch on the books so it shines just above the Equator. It is summer on the half of the ball above the Equator where the torch is shining, and winter on the other half of the world.

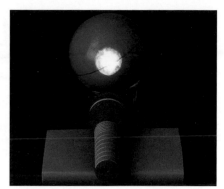

3 Shine the torch on the Equator. It sheds equal light in each hemisphere. This is the equivalent of spring and autumn, when days and nights are of similar length throughout the world.

Solar power ▶

The Sun pours energy on to the Earth as heat and light. The amount of energy received in any one place on the Earth changes with the seasons. This is because the Earth's axis is tilted. In the summer, one half of the Earth tilts towards the Sun, and is warmer. In the winter, it tilts away from the Sun and is colder.

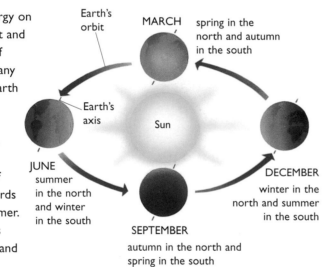

Earth's orbit

MARCH — spring in the north and autumn in the south

Earth's axis

Sun

JUNE summer in the north and winter in the south

DECEMBER winter in the north and summer in the south

SEPTEMBER autumn in the north and spring in the south

Make a thermometer

1 Pour cold water into the bottle until it is about two-thirds full. Add some food colouring. Dip the straw into the water and seal the neck tightly with reusable adhesive.

4 On a hot day, the Sun's heat will make the air and water expand, forcing the water level in the straw above the room temperature mark. Cool the thermometer in the fridge. Mark the different levels.

2 Blow down the straw to force some extra air into the bottle. After a few seconds, the extra air pressure inside will force the water level to rise up the straw.

3 Cut the card and slot it over the straw. Let the bottle stand for a while. Make a mark on the card by the water level to show room temperature. Take your thermometer outside.

Phases of the Moon

The Moon is Earth's closest neighbour in space. We know more about the Moon than about any other heavenly body because astronauts have landed on it and explored the surface. The Moon is Earth's only satellite. It measures 3,476km across, about a quarter of the size of the Earth. It circles around the Earth at a distance of approximately 385,000km, and makes the journey about once a month. The Moon does not give out any light of its own. We see it because it reflects light from the Sun. Sunlight illuminates different parts of the Moon as the month goes by. This makes the Moon seem to change shape. The Moon spins around slowly as it circles the Earth, so the same side is always turned towards the Earth.

We only see the Moon lit up completely once a month, but you do not have to wait a month to see the changes in its shape or phases. The project here will show you in just a few minutes how the Moon goes through its phases!

▲ **Face of the Moon**
This picture shows a view of the Moon from the Earth. When the whole of the Moon is lit up like this, we call it a full Moon. The darker regions on the surface are great dusty plains called seas, or maria. The lighter areas are highlands. These are pitted with craters that are sometimes hundreds of kilometres across. Mountains on the Moon rise to more than 6,000m.

Make your own Moon

YOU WILL NEED

football or beach ball, glue, glue brush, glass, silver paper or foil, scissors, reusable adhesive, torch.

I Make sure that you have washed and dried your ball thoroughly before using! Paint glue all over the ball. Rest it on a glass or something similar to keep it still.

2 Carefully cut the silver paper or foil into large square sheets. Wrap up the ball in the silver paper. Try to ensure that the wrapping is as smooth as possible. You now have your Moon!

3 Place your Moon on a table. Wedge a small ball of reusable adhesive under the ball. This will hold it firm and stop it from rolling off the table.

4 Get your friend to stand at one side of the table to shine a torch with a strong beam on your Moon. Go to the opposite side of the table. Look at your Moon with the main lights out.

5 Gradually move round the table, still looking at your Moon, which is lit up one side by the torch. You will see the different shapes it takes. These shapes are the Moon's phases.

Going through the phases ▸

When you are opposite your friend in the project, the side of the ball facing you is dark. This is what happens once a month in the night sky. We can only see a thin sliver of light, which we call a new or crescent Moon. As you move around the table, more of the ball is lit by the torch. All of it will be lit when you are behind your friend. When this happens to the real Moon, we describe it as full. As you move around, the ball gradually fades into darkness. When you are opposite your friend again you will see a new Moon again.

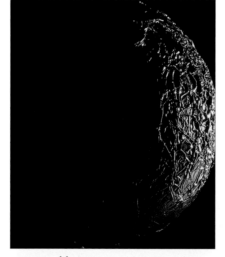

crescent Moon

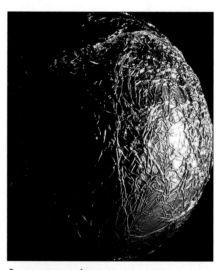

first quarter phase

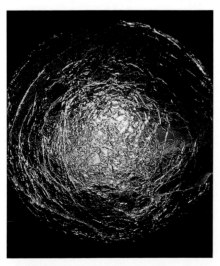

full Moon

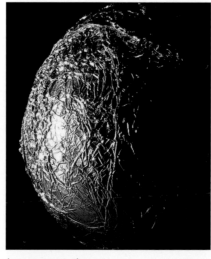

last quarter phase

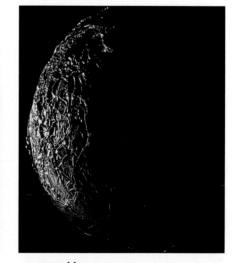

crescent Moon

The rise and fall of tides

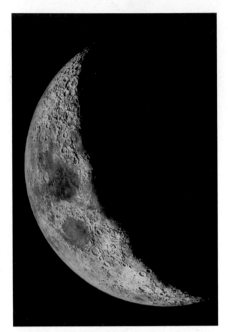

▲ Close neighbour
The Moon is a lifeless desert of rock. It has no atmosphere to protect it from the Sun's dangerous rays, and no water to sustain life. The shape of the Moon appears to change during the month. We call these changes in shape the Moon's phases. It takes the Moon 29½ days to change from a slim crescent to a full circle and back again.

The Earth appears blue from the darkness of Space. This is because more than 70 per cent of its surface is covered with oceans. The seas make up more than one million million million tonnes of seawater.

Every 12 hours or so, the seawater rises then falls back again. These rises and falls are called the tides. When the water is rising, we say the tide is flowing. When it is falling, we say the tide is ebbing. The movement of the ocean waters is caused by the Moon and by the Earth spinning. Gravity pulls the Moon and Earth together. As the Earth turns, the Moon pulls at the ocean water directly beneath it, causing the water to rise. A similar rise in sea level occurs on the opposite side of the Earth, where the water bulges out as a result of the Earth spinning. At these places, there is a high tide. Some six hours later, the Earth has turned 90°. The sea then falls to its lowest point and there is a low tide.

The two experiments opposite explain how the oceans rise and fall without any change in the amount of seawater, and how the tidal bulges of water stay in the same place below the Moon, as the Earth spins beneath it.

How tides occur

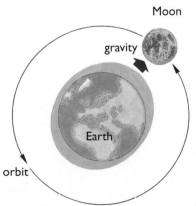

Tides rise beneath the Moon as the Earth turns. The gravity of the Moon tugs at the oceans, pulling the water around with it.

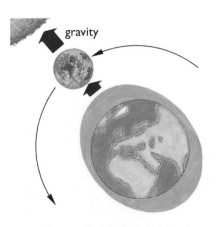

Once every two weeks, the Sun and the Moon line up with the Earth. Their combined pull creates a spring tide, where the tides are higher than usual.

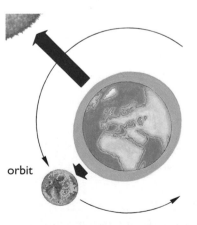

One week later, the Sun and the Moon are at right angles to each other. Pulling in different directions, they create a lower tide than usual, called a neap tide.

High and low tide

1 Place the bowl on a firm, flat surface, then half fill it with water. Place the ball gently in the water so that it floats in the middle of the bowl, as shown in the picture.

2 Place both hands on top of the ball, and push it down into the water gently but firmly. Look what happens to the level of the water. It rises in a 'high tide'.

3 Let the ball gently rise again. Now you can see the water in the bowl dropping again. So the tide has risen and fallen, even though the amount of water is unchanged.

The tidal bulge

YOU WILL NEED

High and low tide: plastic bowl, water, plastic ball to represent the world.

The tidal bulge: strong glue, one 20cm length and two 40cm lengths of thin string, plastic ball to represent the world, plastic bowl, hand drill, water.

1 Glue the 20cm length of the string very firmly to the ball and leave it to dry. Meanwhile, ask an adult to drill two holes in the rim of the bowl, one on each side.

2 Thread a 40cm length of string through each hole and knot the string around the rim. Half fill the plastic bowl with water and float the ball in the water.

3 Ask a friend to pull the string on the ball towards him or her. There is now more water on one side of the ball than the other. This is called a tidal bulge.

4 The Moon pulls on the water as well as the Earth. So now ask the friend to hold the ball in place while both of you pull out the strings attached to the bowl until it distorts.

5 There is now a tidal bulge on each side of the world. One of you slowly turn the ball. Now you can see how, in effect, the tidal bulges move round the world as the world turns.

Ocean waves and currents

▲ Powerful seas
In stormy weather, giant waves rear up and crash down, turning the sea into a raging turmoil.

The sea is rarely still. Even on a calm day, you will see ripples on the surface. Waves move over the ocean's surface. They are driven mainly by the wind. The stronger the winds, and the longer the fetch (the distance they have travelled), the bigger and higher the waves are. Waves usually only affect the surface of the water. As they travel, the water itself does not move. It just moves up and down as the wave passes through it. At a very deep level in some oceans, the water does move in giant streams called ocean currents. These can be hot or cold and can affect the world's climate. Ocean currents are usually caused by differences in the water's saltiness or temperature, rather than by the wind.

The first project shows how waves are made, and the second, how currents are set up by the wind blowing. Currents such as the ones in the third project happen on a much larger scale in the world's major oceans.

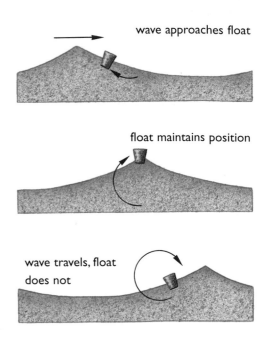

wave approaches float

float maintains position

wave travels, float does not

▲ Wave goodbye
The diagrams above show how waves travel across the water surface, while objects floating on the water hardly move at all.

Making waves

<table>
<tr><td>

YOU WILL NEED

rectangular plastic bowl, jug, water, bath or inflatable paddling pool, non-hardening modelling material.

</td></tr>
</table>

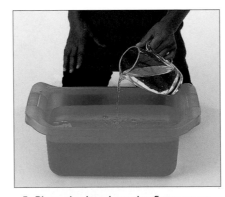

1 Place the bowl on the floor or on a table. Choose a place where it does not matter if a little water spills out. Fill the bowl with water until it almost reaches the brim.

2 Blow very gently over the surface of the water. You will see that the water begins to ripple where you blow on it. This is how ocean waves are formed by air movement.

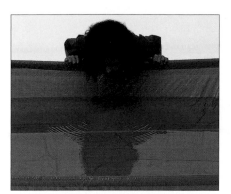

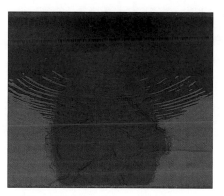

3 Fill the bath or pool with water. Blow gently along the length of the bath or pool. Blow at the same strength as in step 2, and from the same height above the water.

4 Keep blowing for a minute or so. Notice that the waves are bigger in the bath or pool, even though you are not blowing harder. This is because they reach farther across the water.

5 Now drop a small piece of modelling material into the water. Watch how it sets up waves. Ripples travel out in circles from where the modelling material entered the water.

Ocean currents

YOU WILL NEED

rectangular plastic bowl, jug,

water, talcum powder.

I Place the bowl on the floor or on a table. Choose a place where it does not matter if a little water spills out. Fill the bowl with water until it almost reaches the rim.

2 Scatter a small amount of talcum powder over the water. Use just enough powder to make a very fine film over the water's surface. The less you use, the better.

4 Keep blowing and the powder swirls in two circles as it hits the far side. This is what happens when currents hit continents. One current turns clockwise, the other turns anticlockwise.

3 Blow very gently across the water from the centre of one side of the bowl to the other. You will see how the water starts to move. Ocean currents begin to move in the same way.

Changing coastlines

Of all the natural forces that erode (wear away) the land, the sea is the most powerful. It carries sand particles that act like a grindstone on the shore. Waves are forced into cracks in the rocks. They widen the cracks, eventually breaking up the rock face. Huge cliffs are carved out of mountains, broad platforms are sliced back through rocks and houses are left dangling over the edges of the land.

New land can also be created at the ocean's edge. Where headland cliffs are being eroded by waves, the bays between may fill with sand. On coasts where the sea is shallow, waves build beaches of shingle, sand and mud. The first experiment demonstrates the destructive effect of the sea when it hits the shore. The second project shows how waves make ripples on sandy beaches.

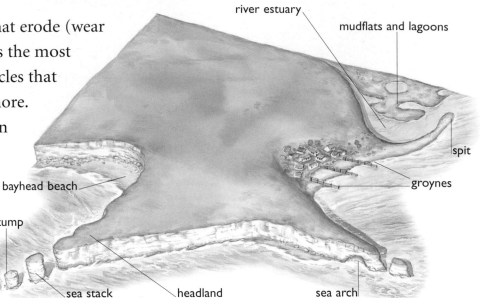

river estuary

mudflats and lagoons

spit

groynes

bayhead beach

stump

sea stack

headland

sea arch

▲ Ever-changing landscape

The sea's power to build and destroy a coastline can be seen in this picture. Coastal areas that are exposed to the full force of the waves are eroded into steep cliffs. Headlands are worn back, leaving behind stacks, stumps and arches. In more sheltered places, the sand piles up to form beaches, or waves may carry material along the coast to build spits and mudflats.

▲ Relentless assault

The sea is at its most spectacular at the edges of big oceans, where the waves are big and powerful. Their continuous assault on the land will, in time, break up the toughest rocks into tiny pieces.

Attacking the shore

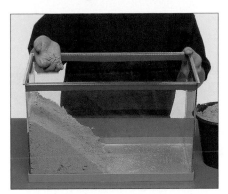

1 Mix a little water with the sand in a bucket until it is quite wet and sticks firmly together. Then pack the sand into a wedge shape at one end of the tank.

2 Carefully pour water into the empty end of the tank so as not to disturb the sand too much. Fill the tank until the water level comes about two-thirds of the way up the sloping sand.

3 Make gentle waves in the water on the side opposite the sand. Notice how the waves gradually wear away the sloping sand. This is what happens on a sandy seashore.

How ripples are formed in sand

YOU WILL NEED
Making waves: sand, plastic bucket, water tank, water, jug.
How ripples are formed in sand: heavy filled round tin, round plastic bowl, jug, water, fine clean sand, spoon.

1 Place a heavy tin in the centre of the plastic bowl, then fill the bowl with water to at least half way. The water should not cover more than two-thirds of the tin.

2 Sprinkle a little sand into the bowl to create a thin layer about ½cm deep. Spread the sand until it is even, then let it settle into a flat layer at the bottom of the bowl.

3 Stir the water gently with the spoon. Drag the spoon in a circle around the tin. As the water begins to swirl, stir faster with the spoon, but keep the movement smooth.

4 As you stir faster, lift the spoon out and let the water swirl around by itself. The sand will start to develop ripples. As you stir faster, the ripples become more defined.

Water on the move

Rivers start high in the hills and wind their way down towards the sea, or sometimes, a lake. At its start, a river is a tiny stream tumbling down the slopes. It is formed by rain running off a mountainside or by water bubbling up from a spring. As the water flows downhill, it is joined by other streams and grows bigger.

The first project shows how water shapes the landscape by physically eroding (wearing away) the rock. The second experiment demonstrates how in some places, erosion can be a chemical process, in which water dissolves the rock and carries it away.

Over millions of years, a river can carve a gorge deep through solid rock, or deposit (lay down) a vast plain of fine mud called silt. The great rivers of the world take millions of tonnes of mud, rock and sand from the land every day and carry them into the sea. If the river meets a low-lying shoreline, the sediment is dropped. It may spread out into a fan-shaped muddy plain called a delta. When this happens, the river is forced to branch out into smaller streams as it flows into the sea. You can see how this happens in the third experiment.

upper reaches

middle reaches

lower reaches

◀ The course of a river
As it moves across the land, a river changes character. In the upper reaches, it is a fast-flowing, tumbling stream cutting down through steep, narrow valleys. Lower down, it broadens and deepens into a river. Eventually it moves across a broad floodplain before reaching the sea.

The destructive power of water

1 Put one end of a baking tray on a brick. Put the other end of the baking tray on a lower tray or bowl, so that it slopes downwards. Make a sandcastle on the baking tray.

2 Slowly drip water over the sandcastle. Watch the sand crumble and form a new shape. This happens because the sand erodes away where the water hits it.

3 Make sure that the water flows down the centre of the baking tray. This way, the water hits the middle of the sand castle, eroding the centre to form a natural stack.

Chemical erosion

YOU WILL NEED

**The destructive power
of water:** baking tray, brick, tray or
bowl, sand, castle mould, jug, water.

Chemical erosion: baking tray,
brown sugar, jug of water.

Making a delta: scissors, long
cardboard container, two plastic bin
liners, sticky tape, trowel, sand,
block of wood, jug of water.

1 Build a pile of brown sugar on a
tray. Imagine that it is a mountain
made of a soluble rock (that dissolves
in water). Press the sugar down firmly
and shape it to a point.

2 Drip water on your sugar
mountain. It will erode as the
water dissolves the sugar. The water
running off should be brown, because
it contains dissolved brown sugar.

Making a delta

1 Use scissors to trim the top of
the cardboard container so that it
is about 10–15cm deep. Now take
the two plastic bin liners to make the
box waterproof.

2 Cover the inside of the box with
the bin liners and tape them
securely at each end of the box.
Make sure that the seal between the
bin liners is secure.

3 Using the trowel, carefully spread
a layer of sand over the bottom of
the tray until the sand is about 4–5cm
deep. Flatten the sand with the trowel
until it is smooth.

4 Rest one end of the container on
a block of wood or something
similar, to make a slope. Pour water
from the jug on to the sand in the
middle of the higher end.

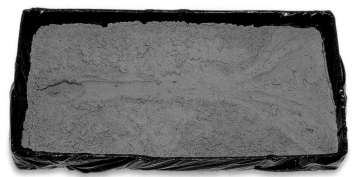

5 If you continue pouring, you will
find that the water gradually
washes away a path through the sand.
It deposits sand it has washed away at
the lower end in a delta region.

Cloud and rain

Water moves around the Earth and its atmosphere in a continuous process called the water cycle. Heat from the Sun causes water from oceans, lakes and rivers to evaporate into water vapour. Water is also released into the atmosphere from plants in a process called transpiration. Flowers and trees take up water from their roots. They use some and release the rest back out through their leaves – water vapour rises into the atmosphere. It cools as it rises, and changes back into tiny droplets of liquid water. This is called condensation. The droplets gather together and form clouds. When the water in the atmosphere becomes too heavy to be held in the air, it returns to the Earth's surface as precipitation (dew, rain, sleet and snow). The land has a fresh supply of water and so the water cycle continues.

The first experiment shows you how water changes to vapour and back again, when a cold surface makes the water vapour condense into water droplets. In the second project you can make a simple rain gauge to measure the amount of rain you get where you live. If you live in a desert region, you may have to wait a long time!

cloud of ice crystals

cloud of water droplets

water vapour rises

▲ Forming clouds

Clouds form when warm air containing water vapour rises into the air and cools. The vapour turns into droplets of water, forming clouds. If the air is very cold, the vapour turns into a cloud of tiny ice crystals.

YOU WILL NEED

heat-proof jug, water, saucepan, oven gloves, plate.

Water vapour

I Fill up the jug with water from the hot tap. Pour the water into the saucepan. Switch on one of the hotplates or light a gas ring on the cooker and place the saucepan on it.

2 Heat the water until it is boiling hard and steam is rising. Lift the plate with the oven gloves. Hold it upside-down above the saucepan. After a few minutes, turn off the heat.

3 Take the plate away, using the oven gloves. You will see that the plate is covered with drops of water. This is water vapour that has cooled and turned back into liquid.

Measuring rainfall

YOU WILL NEED

scissors, sticky paper, large, straight-sided jar, ruler, ballpoint pen, large plastic funnel, notebook, narrow straight-sided jar or glass.

1 Cut a strip of sticky paper the same height as the jar. Stick it on the outside of the jar. Use a ruler and pencil to mark 1cm intervals on the paper strip.

2 Place the funnel in the jar. Put the gauge outside in an open space away from any trees. Look at the gauge at the same time each day. Has it rained in the last 24 hours?

3 If it has rained, use the scale to see how much water is in the jar. This is the rainfall for the past 24 hours. Make a note of the reading. Empty the jar before you return it to its place.

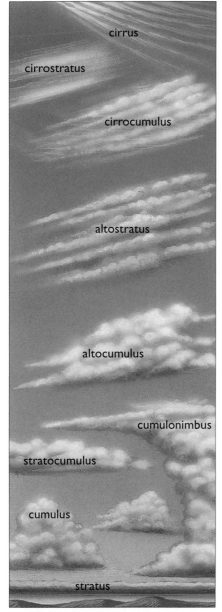

▲ Cloud spotter

cirrus

cirrostratus

cirrocumulus

altostratus

altocumulus

cumulonimbus

stratocumulus

cumulus

stratus

The main kinds of clouds we see in the sky can be grouped according to how far they are above the Earth's surface. High clouds include cirrus clouds. Altostratus and altocumulus are middle clouds. Stratus and cumulus clouds are examples of low clouds.

4 You can measure rainfall more accurately if you use a separate, narrower measuring jar. Stick another strip of sticky paper along the side of this jar. Pour water into the large collecting jar up to the 1cm mark. Then pour the water into the narrow jar. Mark 1cm where the water level reaches. Divide the length from the bottom of the jar to the 1cm mark into 10 equal parts. Each will be equivalent to 1mm of rainfall. You can now extend the scale past the 1cm mark to the top of the narrow jar. Use this jar to measure the rainfall you collect to the nearest millimetre, just as professional meteorologists do.

What is humidity?

The temperature of a place is mainly controlled by the amount of heat it absorbs from the Sun. Another factor is altitude (how high the land is). Areas at very high altitudes are colder than areas at sea level. Distance from the sea also affects temperature. The sea has a moderating effect. You can see how this works in the first project. Water takes more time to heat up than the land, but holds its heat for much longer. Therefore on the coast, summers are cooler and winters milder than inland.

A temperature of 21°C in the Caribbean feels much hotter than 21°C in Egypt. This is due to humidity – the amount of water vapour in the air. When there is high humidity, the air feels moist and sticky. The perspiration on our skin cannot evaporate as there is too much water in the air already. When there is little water vapour in the air, the air feels dry. The perspiration on our skin escapes more easily and cools us down. The second experiment shows you how to measure humidity using a simple device called a hygrometer. When air is very humid, there is more chance that it will rain.

▲ Water from plants

Plants play a vital role in creating humidity. A plant's leaves give off water vapour in a process called transpiration. Cover a pot plant with a clear plastic bag. Seal the plastic around the pot with sticky tape. Put the plant in direct sunlight for two hours. Notice that the bag starts to mist up and droplets of water form on the inside. They form when the water vapour given off by the plant turns back to a liquid.

Measuring temperature changes

YOU WILL NEED

Measuring temperature changes: two bowls, jug of water, sand, watch, thermometer, notebook, pen.

Measuring humidity: two sheets of coloured card, scissors, ruler, pen, glue, toothpick, used matchstick, straw, reusable adhesive, blotting paper, hole punch.

1 Pour water into one bowl and sand into the other bowl. You do not need to measure the exact quantities of sand and water – just use roughly equal amounts.

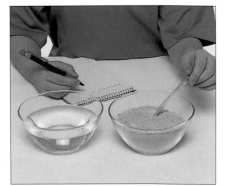

2 Place the bowls side by side in a cool place. Leave them for a few hours. Then note the temperature of the sand and water. The temperature of each should be about the same.

3 Place the bowls side by side in the sunlight. Leave the bowls for an hour or two. Then measure and record the temperatures of the sand and water in each bowl.

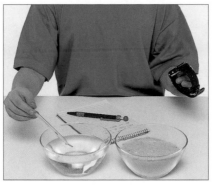

4 Put each bowl in a cool place indoors. Measure and record the temperature of the sand and water every 15 minutes. The sand cools down faster than the water.

5 In this experiment, the sand acts like land and the water acts like the ocean. The sand gets hot quicker, but the water holds its heat longer. Dip your hands in to feel the difference.

Measuring humidity

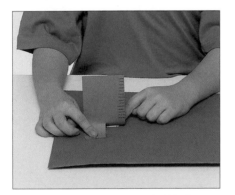

1 Cut out a card rectangle. Mark regular intervals along one side for a scale. Cut a 2cm slit in one short side. Split the parts out as shown above and glue them to a card base.

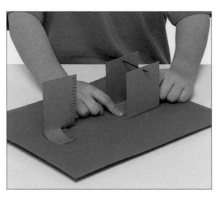

2 Cut another long rectangle from the card. Fold it and stick it to the card base as shown above. Pierce the top carefully with a toothpick to form a pivot.

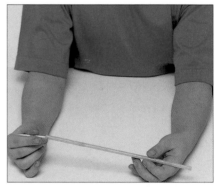

3 Fix the used matchstick to one end of the straw using some reusable adhesive, to make a pointer. Both the matchstick and the adhesive give the pointer some weight.

4 Carefully cut out several squares of blotting paper. Use the hole punch to make a hole in the middle of each square. Slide the squares over the flat end of the pointer.

5 Now carefully pierce the pointer with the toothpick pivot. Position the pointer as shown above. Make sure that the pointer can swing freely up and down.

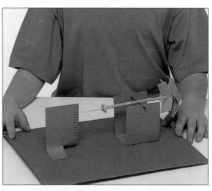

6 Adjust the position of the toothpick so that it stays level. Take the hygrometer into the bathroom and run a bath. The humidity makes the blotting paper damp. The pointer tips upwards.

The way the wind blows

The wind is moving air. Wind can move dust, sand and other small items. The first experiment shows how the weight of a particle affects how far it travels. The wind also brings about changes in the weather. Meteorologists study the wind to help them predict these changes. They use a weather vane to find out its direction. The second project shows how to make a simple weather vane. Wind speed is measured using an anemometer. This device consists of a circle of cups that spin when the wind blows, like a windmill. The faster the wind blows the faster the anemometer spins.

YOU WILL NEED

How wind sorts sand: two empty ice cube trays, piece of card large enough to fit over an ice cube tray, spoon, mix of fine and coarse sand, hairdryer.

Make a weather vane: reusable adhesive, plastic pot and its lid, scissors, garden stick, two plastic straws, coloured card, pen, sticky tape, pin, plywood, compass.

parabolic dune

transverse dune

wind direction

barchan dune

seif dune

◄ Name that dune

Some deserts contain vast seas of sand, called ergs, where the wind piles sand up into dunes. The shape of the dune depends on the amount of sand and changeability of the wind direction. Crescent-shaped dunes called parabolic dunes are common on coasts. Ones with narrow points facing away from the wind are called barchans. These dunes creep slowly forward. Transverse dunes form at right angles to the main wind direction. Seifs occur where there is little sand, and wind comes from different directions.

How wind sorts sand

1 Turn one ice cube tray over, and lay it down end to end with another ice cube tray. Place the card over the upturned tray and spoon the sand over it to make a sand dune.

2 Hold a hairdryer close to the upturned tray, pointing it towards the other tray. Turn the hairdryer on so that it blows sand into the open ice cube tray.

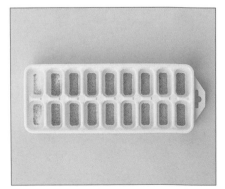

3 Look at the grains in each box. The distance a grain travels depends on its weight. Heavy grains fall in the end of the tray nearest to you. Light grains are blown to the farthest end.

Make a weather vane

1 Stick a ball of reusable adhesive to the middle of the lid of the pot. Ask an adult to pierce a hole in the bottom of the pot with the scissors. Place the pot on top of the lid.

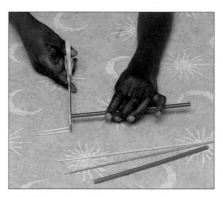

2 Slide the stick into one of the straws. Trim the end of the stick so that it is a little shorter than the straw. Push the straw and stick through the hole in the pot and into the adhesive.

3 Cut out a square of card. Mark each corner with a point of the compass – N, E, S, W. Fold in half and snip a hole in the middle. Carefully slip the card over the straw.

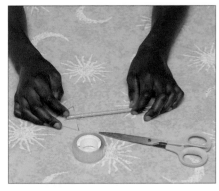

4 Cut out two card triangles. Stick them to each end of the second straw to form an arrow head and tail. Put a ball of reusable adhesive in the top of the first straw in the pot.

5 Push a pin through the middle of the arrow. Stick the pin into the reusable adhesive in the first straw. Be careful not to prick your finger when you handle the pin.

6 Secure your weather vane to a plywood base using a piece of reusable adhesive. Test it for use – the arrow should spin round freely when you blow on it.

7 Take your weather vane outside and use a compass to point it in the right direction. You can now discover the direction the wind is blowing.

Turning the sails ▶

The miniature windmills on this toy spin faster the harder you blow on them. The sails of real windmills also spin faster as the speed of the wind increases. As a result, windmills need a 'governor'. This device regulates the speed of the sails' rotation so they are not damaged in very windy weather.

Recording weather

Meteorologists gather information about the weather from satellites, balloons and other instruments. Powerful computers help them to analyse the data. Using this information, meteorologists draw weather maps. These can show the state of the weather at any one time, or they can be a forecast of weather in the future. The maps use symbols to represent conditions such as rainfall and wind direction.

You can set up your own weather station to record daily conditions with a few simple devices. You will be able to use some of the instruments you have made in other projects, such as the weather vane, hygrometer and rain gauge. You will also need to buy a thermometer to measure the temperature. Take measurements with your weather instruments every day. Write them down in a special weather book. Also, make a note of what the weather is like generally – fine, cloudy, drizzly, frosty and so on. Don't forget to make a note of the date!

Meteorologists look at records from the past to discover changes in climate. The project opposite shows you how to make your own discoveries about climate changes by looking at the record of tree growth.

▲ **Forecasting rain**
A hygrometer will gauge the amount of moisture in the air. When the pointer tilts up on the scale, the air is moist and rain may be on the way.

▲ **Measuring rainfall**
A rain gauge will tell you how much rain has fallen. Rainfall is collected over a set period in a jar or measuring bottle, and the amount is recorded.

▲ **Wind direction**
A windmill shows how hard the wind is blowing. A weather vane will tell you the wind's direction. The arrow points in the direction that the wind is blowing from. So if the arrow points west, the wind is a west wind.

The wooden weather record

YOU WILL NEED

newly cut log, decorator's paintbrush, ruler with millimetre measurements, metric graph paper, pen or pencil.

1 Ask a tree surgeon, the local council or a sawmill for a newly cut slice of log. Use the paintbrush to brush away the dust and dirt from the slice of wood.

2 When the log slice is clean, examine it closely. Look at the pattern of rings. They are small in the centre and get bigger and bigger towards the outer edge of the log.

3 Each ring is a year's growth. So count the rings out from the centre carefully. This tells you how old the tree is. If there are 105 rings, for instance, the tree is 105 years old.

4 Using a ruler, measure the width of each ring. Start from the centre and work outwards. Ask a friend to write down the widths as you call them out.

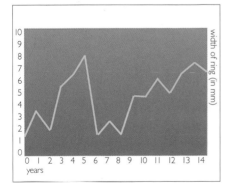

5 On graph paper, mark five squares for each year along the bottom. Mark widths for the rings up the side, five squares for each millimetre. Plot your measurements as dots for each year.

6 Join the dots with a line. This line shows how the weather has changed with each year. If the line is going up, the weather was warmer so the tree grew a lot. If the line falls, the weather was colder so the tree grew less.

25

Restless Earth

The movement of rocks that causes earthquakes usually occurs deep inside the Earth's crust. The exact point at which the rocks start to break or fracture is known as the focus. This can lie as deep as hundreds of kilometres or as close as a few tens of kilometres down. The most violent disturbance on the surface occurs at a point directly above the focus, called the epicentre.

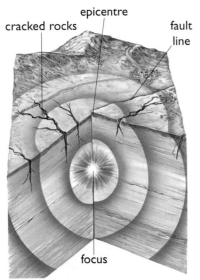

▲ Earthquake alert
Most earthquakes originate in rock many kilometres below the surface, at the focus. The most intense vibrations on the surface are felt immediately above the focus, at the epicentre.

The closer the focus, the more destructive is the earthquake. San Francisco, in California, sits near a line of weakness in the Earth's crust known as the San Andreas Fault. The fault marks the boundary of the eastern Pacific plate and the North American plate. As they try to slide past each other, they make the ground shake violently. Earthquakes and volcanoes occur around the boundaries of all the plates on the Earth's surface.

Tremors

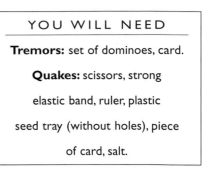

I This project investigates how the energy in earthquake waves (tremors) varies with distance. Near the end of a table, build a simple house out of dominoes. Stand them up on edge.

2 Place the card on the dominoes to make the roof of your house. Many people in earthquake zones live in the simplest of houses, built not too differently from this one.

3 Go to the opposite end of the table and hit it with your hand, but not too hard. Your domino house probably shakes, but still stays standing. Now hit the table at the other end.

4 The waves you create when you hit the table are strong enough to knock down the house. When you hit the other end of the table, the waves are too weak to knock it down.

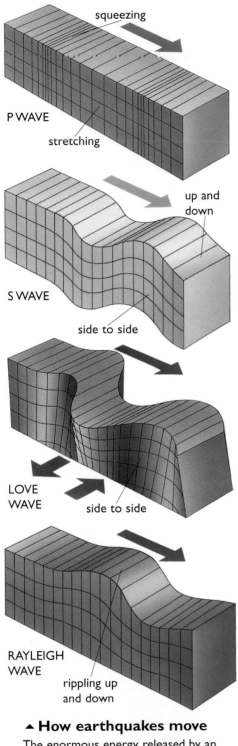

P WAVE

squeezing

stretching

S WAVE

up and
down

side to side

LOVE
WAVE

side to side

RAYLEIGH
WAVE

rippling up
and down

▲ How earthquakes move

The enormous energy released by an earthquake travels through the ground in the form of waves. The P (primary) wave compresses, then stretches rocks it passes through. The S (secondary) wave produces a side-to-side and up-and-down action. Love waves travel on the surface, making the ground move from side to side. Rayleigh waves are surface waves that move up and down.

Quakes

1 With the scissors, cut the elastic band at one end to make a long strip. This represents a layer of rock inside the Earth before it is affected by an earthquake.

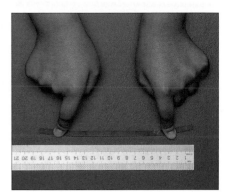

2 Measure the strip of elastic with a ruler. This represents the original length of the rock in the ground. Make a note of how long the elastic is at this stage.

3 Stretch the elastic band and hold it tightly above the tray. In the same way, rocks get stretched by pulling forces inside the Earth during an earthquake.

4 Ask a friend to hold the card on top of the elastic and sprinkle some salt on it. The salt layer on the card represents the surface of the ground above the stretched rock layer.

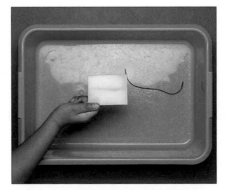

5 Now let go of the ends of the elastic. Notice how the salt grains on the card are thrown about. This was caused by the energy released when the elastic shrank.

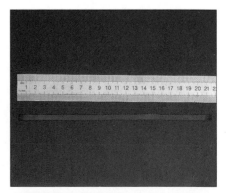

6 Finally, measure the strip of elastic again. You will find that it is slightly longer than it was at the start. Rocks are often permanently stretched a little after an earthquake.

Measuring earthquakes

Scientists who study earthquakes are called seismologists. They have a variety of instruments to gather data. The Newton's cradle experiment below explains how waves (tremors) work. The other projects show two ways in which seismologists detect how ground moves at the beginning of an earthquake. A gravimeter measures small changes in gravity. The tiltmeter detects whether rock layers are tilting.

YOU WILL NEED

Newton's cradle: large beads, lengths of wool, sticky tape, cane, four wooden blocks.

Gravimeter: sticky paper, ruler, pen, large jar, non-hardening modelling material, elastic band, toothpick, pencil.

Newton's cradle

1 Tie the beads to the ends of the wool threads. Tape the other ends to the cane. Make sure the threads are all the same lengths, and that the beads just touch when they hang down.

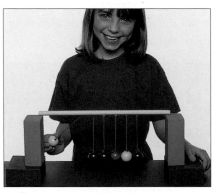

2 Prop up the cane at both ends on a pair of blocks supported by more blocks underneath. Secure the ends of the cane with tape. Lift up the bead at one end of the row and let go.

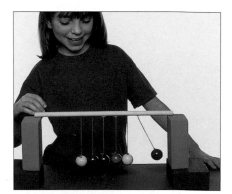

3 The bead at the other end flies up. The energy of the falling bead at one end travels as a pressure wave through the middle ones. It reaches the bead at the other end and pushes it away.

Gravimeter

1 Draw a scale on a strip of sticky paper using a ruler and pen. Stick the scale on the jar. In a real instrument this would measure slight changes in gravity.

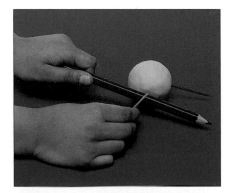

2 Bury one end of an elastic band in a ball of modelling material. Stick in a toothpick at right angles to the band to act as a pointer. Pass the pencil through the loop of the band.

3 Lower the ball into the jar, so the tip of the pointer is close to the scale. Fix the pencil on top with modelling material. Move the jar up or down and the pointer moves down or up the scale.

Tiltmeter

YOU WILL NEED

bradawl (hole punch), two transparent plastic cups, transparent plastic tubing, non-hardening modelling material, pen, sticky paper, ruler, wooden board, adhesive, food colouring, jug of water.

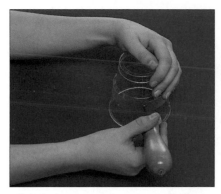

1 Use the bradawl to make a hole in the side of each plastic cup, just about half-way down. Be careful not to prick your fingers. Ask an adult to help you if you prefer.

2 Push one end of the tubing into the hole in one of the cups. Seal it tight with modelling material. Put the other end in the hole in the other cup and seal it as well.

3 Using the pen, draw identical scales on two strips of the sticky paper. Use a ruler and mark regular spaces. Stick the scales at the same height on the side of the cups.

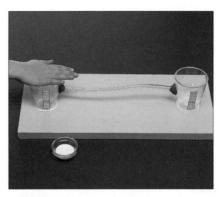

4 Stick the cups to the wooden baseboard with adhesive. Position them so that the tube between is pulled straight, but make sure it doesn't pull out.

6 Your tiltmeter is now ready for use. When it is level, the water levels in the cups are the same. When it tilts, the water levels change as water runs through the tube from one cup to the other. Scientists use tiltmeters to detect whether rock layers are moving by comparing the water levels in two connected containers.

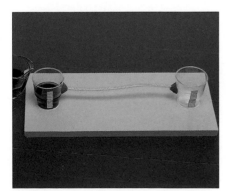

5 Add food colouring to water in the jug, and pour it into each of the cups. Make sure to fill the cups so that the water level reaches over the openings to the tubes.

Do-it-yourself seismograph

There are hundreds of seismic (from the Greek word *seismos*, meaning earthquake) centres around the world. Within minutes of a quake, scientists begin analysing data from their seismographs. They then compare notes with scientists in other countries. The Italian scientist Luigi Palmieri built the first seismograph in 1856. All seismographs work on the same principle. They have a light frame attached to the ground and a heavy weight attached to the frame by a spring. The heavy weight has a high inertia, which means it is more difficult to get moving than a light object. When an earthquake happens, the frame shakes with the ground but the heavy weight stays in the same place because of inertia. The movement of the frame around the steady weight is recorded by a pen on a roll of paper, which draws a wavy line. The same principle of the inertia of a heavy weight is used to detect tremors in the seismograph shown here.

▲ Catching the tremors

The Chinese invented a type of seismograph in AD132. When there was an earthquake, a ball was released from one of the dragons and fell into a frog's mouth. This showed the direction of the vibrations. The instrument detected an earth tremor 500km away.

Building a seismograph

1 The cardboard box will become the frame of your seismograph. It needs to be made of quite stiff card. The open part of the box will be the front of your instrument.

2 Make a hole in what will be the top of the frame with the bradawl. If the box feels flimsy, strengthen it by taping round the corners as shown in the picture.

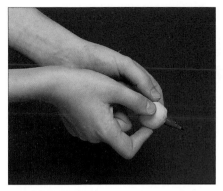

3 Roll a piece of modelling material into a ball and make a hole in it with the pencil. Push the felt-tipped pen through the modelling material to extend a little way beyond the hole.

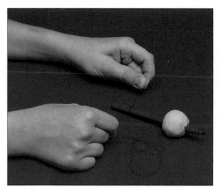

4 This will be the pointer of your seismograph and make a record of earthquake vibrations. Tie one end of the piece of string to the top of the pen.

5 Thread the other end of the string through the hole in the top of the box. Now stand the box upright and pull the string through until the pen hangs free.

6 Tie the top end of the string to the pencil and roll the pencil to take up the slack. When the pen is at the right height (just touching the bottom), tape the pencil into position.

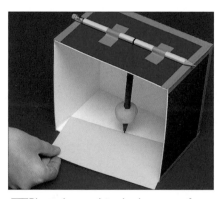

7 Place the card in the bottom of the box underneath the pen. If you have adjusted it properly, the tip of the pen should just touch the card to mark it.

8 Your seismograph is now ready for use. It uses the same principle as a proper seismograph. The heavy bob, or pendulum, will be less affected by shaking motions than the frame.

9 You do not have to wait for an earthquake to test your seismograph. Just shake or tilt the frame. The suspended pen does not move but it marks the piece of card, giving you your very own seismograph.

Slips and faults

Every earthquake, from the slightest tremor to the violent shaking that destroys buildings, has the same basic cause. Two plates of rock grind past each other along a fault line where the Earth's crust has fractured. Friction between the plates means they do not slide past each other smoothly, but jam and then jump. The first experiment on the page opposite shows how friction at fault lines causes great destructive energy.

direction of movement

fault plane

Tectonic (or crustal) plates float on top of the mantle beneath. The oceanic crust is heavier and denser than the continental crust so it sits lower down. The experiment below demonstrates this.

There are several kinds of fault. When blocks slide past each other horizontally, it is called a transform, or strike-slip fault. In a normal fault, the rocks are pulling apart and one block slides down the other. In a thrust fault, the blocks are pressing together, causing one to ride up above the other. The second project on the opposite page shows how these movements create landforms, such as mountains and valleys.

▲ Making mountains

Fault mountains form by the slow, unstoppable movement of tectonic plates. This puts rocks under such huge stress that they sometimes crack. Such cracks are called faults. Where they occur, huge blocks of rock slip up and down past each other, creating cliffs. In places a whole series of giant blocks may be thrown up together, creating a new mountain range. The Black Mountains in Germany are an example of block mountains formed in this way.

Floating plates

YOU WILL NEED
wooden block, polystyrene block, bowl of water

1 The two blocks should be roughly the same size and shape. Polystyrene represents the continental crust, wood the oceanic crust and water the fluid mantle.

2 Place the blocks in the water. The polystyrene floats higher, because it is less dense, just as the continental crust floats higher on the mantle. Which of the two blocks weighs more?

Fault movements

1 Hold a block in each hand so that the sides of the blocks are touching. Pushing gently, try to make the blocks slide past each other. You will find this quite easy.

2 Wet the sides of the blocks with the oil, and try to slide them again. You should find that it is easier because the oil has lessened the friction between the blocks.

3 Pin sheets of sandpaper on the sides of the blocks and try to make them slide now. You will find it much harder. The sandpaper is rough and increases friction between the blocks.

Building mountains

YOU WILL NEED

Fault movements: two wooden blocks, baby oil, drawing pins, sheets of sandpaper.

Building mountains: 20cm square sheet of paper, non-hardening modelling material in various colours, rolling pin, modelling tool.

1 On the sheet of paper, roll out several flat sheets of modelling material, each one a different colour. The sheets should be about the same size as the sheet of paper.

2 Place the square, flat sheets of modelling material on top of each other to make a layered block. The differently coloured layers are like the layers of rock strata in the Earth's crust.

3 Lay the layered block flat on the table. With a modelling tool, carefully make two cuts in the clay – one towards the left and the other towards the right, as shown above.

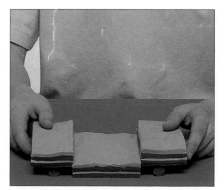

4 Make two small balls. Lift each of the outside pieces that you have cut on to a ball, as shown above. This forms a block mountain separated by a rift valley.

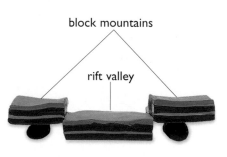

block mountains

rift valley

The crust breaks away at a rift zone where the plates are moving apart. Uplifted rock strata form block mountains, while a descending mass of rock creates the valley.

Building fold mountains

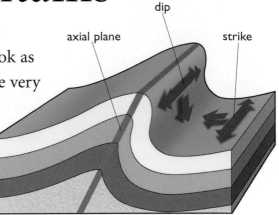

Most high mountains are part of great ranges that stretch for hundreds of kilometres. They may look as if they have been there forever, but geologically they are very young. They have all been thrown up in the last few hundred million years.

The biggest – and youngest – mountain ranges in the world, such as the Himalayas and the Andes, are fold mountains. They started life as flat layers of rock called strata. Layers of rock are laid down over millennia. Some strata form as successive layers of sediments such as sand, mud and seashells settle on the ocean floor. Other strata may be made up of molten rock thrown up from the heart of the Earth by volcanoes.

Fold mountains are layers of rock which have been crunched up by pressure – in a similar way to the pressure you will be exerting in these two projects. In real mountain formation, two of the tectonic plates that make up the Earth's surface push against each other, forcing the rock layers along their edges into massive folds. As the layers of rock are squeezed the folds become more exaggerated.

▲ **Anatomy of a fold**

Geologists describe an upfold as an anticline and a downfold as a syncline. The dip is the direction the fold is sloping. The angle of dip is how steep the slope is. The strike is the line along the fold. The axial plane is an imaginary line through the centre of the fold – this may be vertical, horizontal or at any angle in between.

YOU WILL NEED
thin rug

Simple folds

1 Find an uncarpeted floor and lay the rug down with one short, straight edge up against a wall. Make sure the long edge of the rug is at a right angle to the wall.

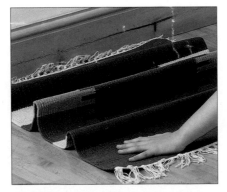

2 Now push the outer edge of the rug towards the wall. See how the rug crumples. This is how rock layers buckle to form mountains, as tectonic plates push against each other.

3 Push the rug up against the wall even more and you will see some of the folds turn right over on top of each other. These are like folded-over strata or layers, called nappes.

Complex folds

YOU WILL NEED

rolling pin, non-hardening modelling
material in various colours,
modelling tool, two blocks of
5cm square wood, two bars
of 10 x 5cm wood.

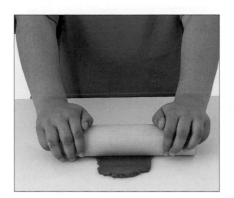

1 Roll out the modelling material into flat sheets in different colours, each about 0.5cm thick. Cut into strips about the same width as the blocks of wood. Square off the ends.

2 Lay the strips carefully one on top of the other, in alternating colours or in a series of colours. These strips represent the layers or strata of rock.

3 Place the blocks of wood at either end of the strips. Lay the bars of wood down on either side of the strips to prevent them from twisting sideways.

4 Ask a friend to hold on to one block, while you push the other towards it. As you push, the effect is similar to two tectonic plates slowly pushing together.

5 From time to time, stop and pull away the bars of wood so that you can have a look at what is happening. As you push harder, see how the layers crumple increasingly and start to turn over themselves. Overlapping folds like this are called nappes.

Fire down below

Volcanoes begin many kilometres beneath the Earth's surface. The landscape that makes up the surface of our planet is only a thin 'crust' of hard rock compared with what lies beneath. First, there is a thick layer of semi-liquid rock called the mantle. Then comes an intensely hot core of iron and nickel. This reaches temperatures of 3,700°C, but the surrounding pressure is so great that it cannot melt.

Heat moves out from the core to the mantle. Here, rocks are semi-liquid and move like treacle. They cannot melt completely because of pressure.

In some parts of the upper mantle, though, rocks do melt and are known as magma. This collects in chambers, and may bubble up through gaps in the crust via a volcano. You can watch how solids such as magma react to heat – become soft, then melt, and finally flow – in this project.

Most of the world's volcanoes lie along fault lines, where plates (sections of the Earth's crust) meet. A few, however, such as those in Hawaii, lie over hot spots beneath the Earth's crust. A hot spot is an area on a plate where hot rock from the mantle bubbles up underneath. The plate above moves but the hot spot stays in the same place in the mantle. The hot spot keeps burning through the plate to make a volcano in a new place. A string of inactive (dead) volcanoes is left behind as the plate moves over the hot spot. Some form islands above the ocean surface. Others, called sea mounts, remain submerged.

mantle

outer core

inner core

crust

continent

ocean

▲ Inside the Earth

Our planet is made up of different layers. The top layer is the hard crust. It is thinnest under the oceans, where it is only about 5–10km thick. Underneath the crust is a thick layer of semi-liquid rock known as the mantle. Beneath the mantle is a layer of liquid metal, mainly iron and nickel, that makes up the Earth's outer core. The inner core at the centre is solid, made up of iron and other metals.

chains of dead volcanoes

active volcano

ocean plate moves

Volcano chain ▶

Magma breaks through the surface plate. As the plate moves, a new part moves over the hot spot. A new volcano forms and the old one dies.

ocean plate

hot spot

Magma temperature

YOU WILL NEED

block of hard cooking margarine, jam jar, jug, hot water, large mixing bowl, stopwatch.

1 Scoop out some margarine and drop it on to the bottom of the jar. For the best results, use hard cooking margarine, rather than a soft margarine spread.

2 Pick up the jar and tilt it slightly. See what happens to the margarine. The answer is, not a lot. It sticks to the bottom of the jar and does not slide down.

3 Fill the jug with hot water and pour some into the bowl. Shake it around to heat the bowl, then pour it away. Now pour the rest of the hot water into the bowl.

4 Pick up the jar and tilt it again. The margarine still will not move. Now place the jar on the bottom of the bowl. Keep your fingers clear of the hot water.

5 Start the stopwatch and after one minute, take out the jar. Tilt it and see if the margarine moves. Return it to the bowl and after another minute, look at it again.

6 Continue to check the jar for a few more minutes. After about a minute, the margarine will slide along the bottom of the jar as it warms and starts to melt. After several minutes, it is quite fluid. Rocks in the upper mantle of the Earth react to heat in a similar way to the margarine.

39

Moving magma

The temperature of the rocks in the Earth's mantle can be as high as 1,500°C. At this temperature the rocks would normally melt, but they are under such pressure from the rocks above them that they cannot melt completely. They are, however, able to flow slowly. This is rather like the solid piece of modelling material in the experiment below that flows slightly when you put enough pressure on it. This kind of flow is called plastic flow. In places, the rocks in the upper part of the mantle do melt completely. This melted rock, called magma, collects in huge pockets called magma chambers. The magma rises because it is hotter and lighter than the semi-liquid rocks. Volcanoes form above magma chambers when the hot magma can rise to the surface. The second project demonstrates this principle using hot and cold water.

▲ **Surprise eruption**
Mount St Helens, in the north-east USA, lies in a mountain range that includes many volcanoes. Until 1980, Mount St Helens had not erupted in 130 years.

◄ **Flowing like rock**
Underneath the Earth's hard crust, the rock is semi-liquid and moves slowly. It flows in currents. Hot rock moves upwards and cooler rock sinks down.

YOU WILL NEED
non-hardening modelling material, wooden board.

Plastic flow

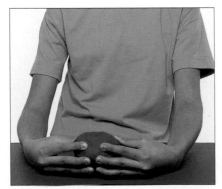

1 Make sure that the table is protected by a sheet. Knead the lump of modelling material in your hands until it is quite flexible. Make it into a ball and place on the table.

2 Place the board on top and press down. The modelling material flattens and squeezes out. It is just like semi-liquid rock flowing under pressure. Make it into a ball again.

3 Press it with the board. Push the board forwards at the same time. The modelling material will flow and allow the board to move forwards like the plates in the Earth's crust.

Rising magma

YOU WILL NEED

dark food colouring, small jar, small jug, transparent plastic food wrapping, scissors, strong elastic band, sharpened pencil, large jar, oven gloves, large jug.

1 Pour some of the food colouring into the small jar. You may need to add more later to give your solution a deep colour. This will make the last stage easier to see.

2 Fill the small jug with water from the hot tap. Pour it into the small jar. Fill it right to the brim, but not to overflowing. Wipe off any that spills down the sides.

Watch what happens. The coloured hot water begins rising from the holes. This happens because the hot water is lighter, or less dense, than the cold water around it. Magma also rises because it is less dense than the semi-liquid rock surrounding it.

3 Cut a circular patch from the plastic food wrapping a few centimetres bigger than the top of the small jar. Place it over the top and secure it with the elastic band.

4 With the sharp end of the pencil, carefully make two small holes in the plastic covering the top of the jar. If any coloured water splashes out, wipe it off.

5 Now place the small jar inside the larger one. Use oven gloves because it is hot. Fill the large jug with cold water and pour it into the large jar, not into the small one.

Erupting volcanoes

Volcanoes are places where molten (liquid) rock pushes up from below through splits in the Earth's crust. The word volcano comes from Vulcan, the name of the ancient Roman god of fire. Vulcanology is the term given to the study of volcanoes and the scientists who study them are known as vulcanologists.

People usually think of volcanoes as producing molten rock. But volcanoes emit much more than just lava. The hot rock inside volcanoes produces many kinds of gases, such as steam and carbon dioxide. Some of these gases go into the air outside the volcano and some are mixed with the lava that flows from it. The project opposite shows you how to make a volcano that gives out lava mixed with carbon dioxide. As you will see, the red floury lava from your volcano comes out frothing, full of bubbles of this gas. In a real volcano, it is the gas that is mixed with the lava that makes the volcano suddenly explode.

▲ **Spectacular explosion**
This gigantic volcano has erupted with explosive violence. Huge clouds of rock and ash have been blasted into the air and rivers of red-hot lava cascade down its slopes. Explosive volcanoes have magma inside them that is full of gas. Gas bubbles swell inside the volcano to push out a mixture of lava and gas violently.

◄ **Forming a cone**
When an explosive volcano erupts, magma (red-hot molten rock) forces its way to the Earth's surface. It shoots into the air along with clouds of ash and gas, and runs out over the sides of the volcano. In time, layers of ash and lava build up to form a huge cone shape. Quiet volcanoes (those which do not explode because their magma contains very little gas) form a different shape.

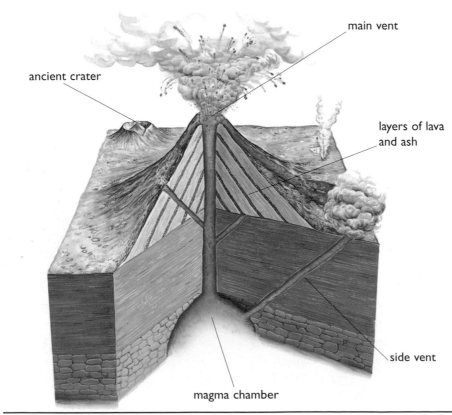

ancient crater

main vent

layers of lava and ash

side vent

magma chamber

Eruption

YOU WILL NFED

jug, baking soda, flour, stirring rod,

funnel, plastic bottle, sand, seed tray

(without holes), large plastic tray,

vinegar, red food colouring.

1 Make sure the jug is dry, or the mixture will stick to the sides. Empty the baking soda into the jug and add the flour. Thoroughly mix the two using the stirrer.

2 Place the funnel in the neck of the plastic bottle. Again, make sure that the funnel is perfectly dry first. Now pour in the mixture of soda and flour from the jug.

3 Empty sand into the tray until it is half-full. Fill the jug with water and pour it into the tray to make the sand sticky but not too wet. Mix together with the stirring rod.

4 Stand the bottle containing the flour and soda mixture in the centre of the plastic tray. Then start packing the wet sand around it. Make the sand into a cone shape.

The sandy volcano you have made will begin to erupt. The vinegar and soda mix to give off carbon dioxide. This makes the flour turn frothy and forces it out of the bottle as red lava.

5 Pour the vinegar into the jug. Then add enough food colouring to make the vinegar a rich red colour. White wine vinegar will make a richer colour than malt vinegar.

6 Place the funnel in the mouth of the plastic bottle and quickly pour into it the red-coloured vinegar in the jug. Now remove the funnel from the bottle.

Volcanic shapes

Some parts of the world have ancient lava (molten rock) flows that are hundreds of kilometres long. Flows such as these have come from fissures (cracks) in the crust, which have poured out runny lava. This lava is much thinner than the lava produced by explosive volcanoes, which is sometimes called pasty lava. Scientists use the term viscosity to talk about how easily a liquid flows. Thin, runny liquids have a low viscosity, and thick liquids a high viscosity. The project shows the viscosities of two liquids and how quickly they flow.

Heating solids to a sufficiently high temperature makes them melt and flow. Rock is no exception to this rule. Deep inside a volcano, hot rock becomes liquid and flows out on to the surface as lava. Its temperature can be as high as 1,200°C. Volcanoes grow in various shapes depending on how runny or thick the lava is.

Submarine (undersea) volcanoes may grow in size until they rise above the surface of the sea.

Fissure volcanoes are giant cracks in the ground from which lava flows.

Shield volcanoes have runny lava and gentle slopes.

Vulcanian volcanoes produce thick, sticky lava and erupt with violent explosions.

Strombolian volcanoes spit out lava bombs in small explosions.

Plinian volcanoes produce thick, gassy lava and shoot columns of ash high into the air.

Lava viscosity

YOU WILL NEED

two paper plates, pen, saucer, jar of
liquid honey, tablespoon, stopwatch,
jug of washing-up liquid.

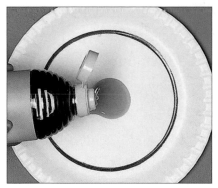

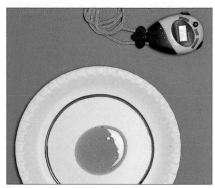

1 Mark a large circle on each plate
by drawing around the edge of
a saucer. Pour a tablespoon of honey
from the jar into the middle of one
of the circles. Start the stopwatch.

2 After 30 seconds, mark with the
pen how far the honey has run.
After another 30 seconds mark again.
Stop the watch when the honey has
reached the circle.

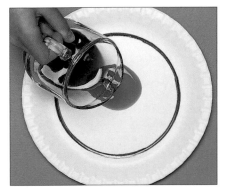

3 Part-fill the jug with washing-up
liquid and pour some into the
centre of the other plate. Use the
same amount as the honey you
poured. Start the stopwatch.

After 30 seconds, note how
far the liquid has run. You
will probably find that it
has already reached the
circle. It flows faster
because it has a much
lower viscosity than honey.

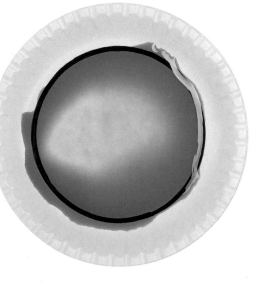

◀ Fast-flowing river

A river of molten lava flows down the
slopes of the volcano Kilauea on the
main island of Hawaii. Like the other
volcanoes on the island, Kilauea is a
shield volcano. It pours out very runny
lava that flows for long distances, usually
at speeds up to about 100m an hour.
The fastest lava flows are called by their
Hawaiian name of pahoehoe.

Vicious gases

▲ Blast off
An enormous cloud of thick ash billows from the top of Mount St Helens, in the USA. The volcano erupted on 18 May 1980. The ash cloud rose to a height of more than 20km.

The experiments here look at two effects that the gases given out by volcanoes can have. In the first project you can see how the build up of gas pressure can inflate a balloon. If you have put too much gas-making mixture in the bottle, the balloon may explode. Be careful! When the gas pressure builds up inside a volcano, an enormous explosion takes place, often releasing a deadly hot gas cloud.

Volcanoes often give out the gas carbon dioxide. This is heavier than air, so a cloud of carbon dioxide descends, pushing air out of the way. Carbon dioxide can kill people and animals. They suffocate because the cloud of carbon dioxide has replaced the air, so oxygen cannot reach their lungs. The second project shows the effect of carbon dioxide. The candle needs oxygen to burn, just as we need it to breathe. Carbon dioxide replaces the air, so the candle goes out.

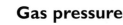

YOU WILL NEED

funnel, drinks bottle, baking soda, vinegar, jug, balloon.

The balloon starts to blow up because of the pressure, or force, of the gas in the bottle. The more gas given out, the more the balloon fills. Don't pop the balloon!

Gas pressure

1 Place the funnel in the top of the bottle and pour in some baking soda. Make sure the funnel is dry or the baking soda will stick to it. Pour the vinegar into the bottle using the funnel.

2 Remove the funnel. Quickly fit the neck of the balloon over the top of the bottle. Notice that the vinegar and soda are fizzing and giving off bubbles of gas.

Suffocating gas

YOU WILL NEED

funnel, bottle, baking soda, vinegar, jug, non-hardening modelling material, pencil, long straw, tall and short candles, large jar, matches.

1 Place the funnel in the bottle and add the baking soda. Pour in the vinegar from the jug. This bottle is your gas generator. The gas produced is carbon dioxide.

2 Knead a piece of modelling material until it is soft, then push it into the mouth of the bottle. Make sure it fits tightly. This will keep the gas from escaping.

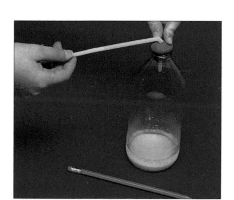

3 Make a hole in the clay stopper with the pencil. Carefully push the straw through the hole, so that it hangs down into the bottle. Press the modelling material around the straw.

4 Stand both candles in the bottom of the large jar. Ask an adult to light them. Light the short one first to avoid the danger of being burned if the tall candle were lit first.

5 Direct the straw of your gas generator into the bottom of the jar. Keep your arms well away from the candle flames. Soon you will find that the short candle goes out. The carbon dioxide gas has covered it and blocked out the oxygen that would let it burn.

▲ A record of the past

Gas killed many of the victims at the Roman town of Pompeii. In AD79 Pompeii was buried by avalanches of hot ash and rock from the erupting Vesuvius. Archaeologists have recreated the shapes of people and animals who died there. They filled hollows left by the bodies with wet plaster of Paris and let it harden. Then they removed the cast from the lava that had covered the bodies.

Steaming hot

In some places in the world, often near plate boundaries, there is magma (hot molten rock) quite near the Earth's surface. This causes other volcanic features such as geysers and hot springs, called geothermal features. The word comes from geo meaning the Earth and thermal meaning heat.

Water from the Earth's surface trickles down through holes and cracks in the land. Geothermal features are almost always caused by magma affecting underground water.

The most spectacular geothermal feature is the geyser. This is a fountain of steam and water that erupts from holes in the ground. Vents (holes) called fumaroles, where steam escapes gently, are more common. Geysers and fumaroles may also give out carbon dioxide and sulphurous fumes.

Hot water can also mix with cooler water to create a hot spring, or with mud to form a bubbling mud hole. Water becomes heated in underground rocks to a temperature above body heat (about 37°C). Some hot springs can be twice this hot. Many are rich in minerals. For centuries, people have believed that bathing in these mineral-rich springs is good for health.

The first experiment on the opposite page shows you how to make a geyser using air pressure to force out water. Blowing into the top of the bottle increases the air pressure there. This forces the coloured water out of the bottle through the long straw. In the second project, you can create a mud hole and discover the sort of bubbles that form in them.

◄ **Regular show**
One of the most famous geysers in the world is Old Faithful, in Yellowstone National Park in Wyoming, USA. This geyser erupts regularly about once every 45 minutes. Yellowstone is the most significant geothermal region in the USA. The National Park also boasts the world's tallest geyser, known as Steamboat. Its spouting column has been known to reach more than 115m.

Geyser eruption

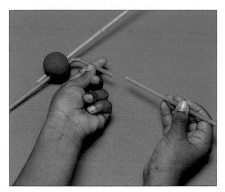

1 Make two holes in a little ball of modelling material and push two bendy straws through it, as shown. Push another straw through the end of one of the first two straws.

2 Pour water into the jug and add the colouring. Then pour it into the bottle. Push the stopper into the neck so that the lengthened straw dips into the coloured water.

3 Place the jar under the other end of the lengthened straw and blow into the other straw. Water spurts into the jar. If the long straw was upright, the water would spout upward like a geyser.

Mudbaths

1 Mix together two tablespoons of cornflour and two of chocolate powder in the bowl, using the wooden spoon. Stir the mixture thoroughly until it is an even colour.

2 Pour about 300ml of milk into the saucepan, and heat it slowly on a hotplate. Keep the hotplate on a low setting to make sure the milk does not boil. Do not leave it unattended.

3 Add some cold milk, little by little, to the mixture of cornflour and chocolate in the bowl. Stir vigorously until the mixture has become a thick smooth cream.

4 Pour the creamy mixture into the hot milk in the saucepan. Hold the handle of the saucepan with the oven glove and stir to stop the liquid sticking to the bottom.

5 If you have prepared your flour and chocolate mixture well, you will now have a smooth, hot liquid looking something like liquid mud. Soon it will start sending up thick bubbles.

The thick bubbles in the mixture will burst with gentle plopping sounds. This is exactly what happens in hot mud pools in volcanic areas.

Volcanic rocks

The lava that flows out of volcanoes eventually cools, hardens and becomes solid rock. Different sorts of lava form different kinds of rocks.

In the first project we see how keeping a liquid under pressure stops gas from escaping. The magma (molten rock) in volcanoes usually has a lot of gas dissolved in it. As it rises through the volcano, the gases start to expand. They help push the magma up and out if the vent is clear. If the vent is blocked, the gas pressure builds up and eventually causes the volcano to explode. The lava that comes from volcanoes with gassy magma forms rock riddled with holes. In some explosive volcanoes, the lava contains so much gas that it forms pumice. This rock is so frothy and light that it floats on water.

When rising magma becomes trapped underground, it forces its way into gaps in the rocks and between the rock layers. This process is known as intrusion and is demonstrated by the second project. The rocks that form when the magma cools and solidifies are called intrusive rocks. Granite is the most common intrusive rock. Often the heat of the intruding magma changes the surrounding rocks. They turn into what are called metamorphic (changed form) rocks.

Sedimentary rocks, such as sandstone, form from the fragments of other rocks that have been broken down by the action of rain, snow, ice and air. The fragments are carried far away by wind or water and settle in a different place.

At some hot parts of the Earth beneath the crust, huge pockets of liquid rock (magma) form. The magma rises, cools and solidifies to form igneous rocks such as granite. If magma reaches the surface of the Earth, it erupts as lava.

Within the Earth, the heat and pressure sometimes become so great that the surrounding rocks are changed. The new rocks are called metamorphic rocks. Marble is formed this way. It comes from limestone rock.

Dissolved gas

1 Stand the jar in the bowl. Pour cold water into the jar from the jug until the jar is nearly full to the top. Break up two antacid tablets and drop them into the jar.

2 Quickly screw the lid on the jar. Little bubbles will start to rise from the tablets but will soon stop. Pressure has built up in the jar and prevents any more gas escaping.

3 Now quickly unscrew the lid from the jar and see what happens. The whole jar starts fizzing. Removing the lid releases the pressure, and the gas in the liquid bubbles out.

Igneous intrusions

1 Make a hole in the bottom of the plastic jar with a bradawl, enough to fit the neck of the toothpaste tube in. Keep your steadying hand away from the sharp end of the bradawl.

2 Place the pieces of broken tiles on the bottom of the jar. Keep them as flat as possible. They are meant to represent the layers of rocks that are found in the Earth's crust.

3 Flatten out the modelling material into a disc as wide as the inside of the jar. Put the disc of modelling material inside the jar. Push it down firmly on top of the tiles.

4 Unscrew the top of the toothpaste tube and force the neck into the hole you have made in the bottom of the bottle. You may have to widen it a little to get the neck in.

5 Squeeze the toothpaste tube hard enough for the toothpaste to come out of the tube. You will see the toothpaste pushing, or intruding, into the layers of tile and making the disc on top rise. Molten magma often behaves in the same way. It intrudes into rock layers and makes the Earth's surface bulge.

Making crystals

Everything around you is made up of tiny particles called atoms. Crystals consist of atoms that are arranged in a regular repeating pattern. This gives the crystal its fixed outer shape. Most solid substances, including metals and minerals found in rocks, are in crystal form.

Igneous rocks are usually made of crystals that form as hot magma (molten rock) cools and solidifies. Crystals may also grow when a water solution containing minerals on the surface of the Earth evaporates. These two ways are demonstrated in the first two experiments.

The type of crystals that form depend on the substances that are dissolved in the liquid. Each mineral forms crystals with a characteristic shape. You can compare the crystals from the first two projects, which use two different solutions. The final experiment demonstrates how atoms are arranged in a crystal. In a liquid, the atoms are loosely joined together and can move about, which is why a liquid flows. As a liquid solidifies, the atoms join together in a regular pattern, like a pyramid, to form a crystal. When atoms are arranged in a disorderly way, they produce a gas.

▲ Making crystals
Place a drop of water on a small, dry mirror and then put it in the freezer. The water will freeze into crystals which can be seen with a hand lens.

YOU WILL NEED
water, measuring jug, saucepan, sugar, tablespoon, wooden spoon, glass jar.

Growing crystals from sugar solution

1 Ask an adult to heat half a litre of water in a saucepan until it is hot, but not boiling. Using a tablespoon, add sugar to the hot water until no more sugar will dissolve in the solution.

2 Stir the solution well, then allow it to cool. When it is quite cold, pour the solution from the pan into a glass jar and put it somewhere where it will not be disturbed.

After a few days or weeks, the solution starts to evaporate and the sugar in the solution will gradually begin to form crystals. The longer it is undisturbed, the larger your crystals will grow.

Growing crystals from washing soda

YOU WILL NEED

Growing crystals from washing soda: jug, hot water, washing soda (sodium carbonate), spoon, bowl, straw, cotton thread, paper clip, hand lens.

Make a model crystal: small, shallow tray (such as the lid of a shoebox), marbles of five different colours.

1 Get an adult to pour about 250ml of very hot water into a jug. Add a spoonful of washing soda. Stir until it all dissolves. Add more soda until no more will dissolve.

2 Dissolving a solid in a liquid makes a solution. Your solution is said to be saturated because no more solid will dissolve. Pour the solution into a bowl, leaving any undissolved solids in the jug.

3 A crystal needs somewhere to start growing. Use a piece of cotton to attach the paper clip to the straw. The distance from straw to clip should be about two-thirds the depth of the bowl.

4 Balance the straw on top of the bowl to let the paper clip dangle in the water. As time goes by, water evaporates leaving crystals on the paper clip.

5 After several days, remove the clip and crystals from the solution and wash them under the cold tap. Look at the crystals through a hand lens. The shapes of your crystals are all the same.

Make a model crystal

1 Fit a layer of blue marbles into the tray in a square pattern. Each central atom is surrounded by eight others. (In some substances, atoms are arranged in a hexagon – a six-sided shape.)

2 Add a second layer. Each marble sits in a dip between four marbles in the layer below. Add a third layer. Each marble is directly above a marble in the first layer.

3 Add two more layers of marbles to make up a complete model crystal. The model crystal you have made is the shape of a square pyramid because you used a square tray.

Glass and bubbles

Igneous rocks start off deep within the Earth as magma (molten rock). The word igneous means 'of fire'. Magma rises towards the surface where it may erupt as lava from a volcano, or cool and solidify within the Earth's crust as igneous rock. Rocks formed in this way are a mass of interlocking crystals, which makes them very strong and ideal as building stones.

The size of the crystals in an igneous rock depends on how quickly the magma cooled. Lavas that cool quickly contain very small crystals. Basalt and andesite are two common kinds of fine-grained igneous rocks, with small crystals. Other rocks, such as granite, cooled more slowly because they solidified inside the Earth's crust. These have a grainy texture because the crystals had time to grow.

The experiments opposite show how igneous rocks can be grainy, or smooth and glassy. They use sugar to represent magma. Sugar melts at a low enough temperature for you to experiment with, but it will still be very hot , so ask an adult to help you carry out these projects. To make real magma, you would need to heat rock up to around 1,000°C until it melted! You can also make the sugar mixture into bubbly honeycomb, a form similar to pumice stone.

▲ **Basalt**
Dark, heavy basalt is one of the most common volcanic rocks. It is formed from the thin, runny lava that pours out of some volcanoes. This sample is known as vesicular basalt because it is riddled with vesicles (holes).

▲ **Andesite**
Lava from explosive volcanoes is thicker and less runny. It can form andesite, which is a lighter-coloured rock than basalt. Andesite is so-called because it is the typical rock found in the Andes Mountains in Peru.

honeycomb (pumice)   toffee (obsidian)   fudge (granite)

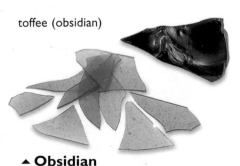

▲ **Pumice**
The bubbles in honeycomb are like those in pumice. Pumice is a very light rock that is full of holes. It forms when lava containing a lot of gas pours out of underwater volcanoes.

▲ **Obsidian**
Glassy toffee cools too rapidly to form crystals. Obsidian is a volcanic rock that is formed when lava cools very quickly. It looks like black glass and is often called volcanic glass.

▲ **Granite**
Fudge's grainy texture is similar to granite. The crystals are large because they grew slowly as the magma cooled slowly. Rhyolite is a kind of granite with smaller crystals and sharp edges.

Crystalline rock

1 Ask an adult to heat 500g of sugar with a little water in a pan. Continue heating until the mixture turns brown, but not black, then add a dash of milk. Leave the mixture to cool.

2 After an hour, you should see tiny crystal grains in the fudge mixture. Once it is completely cool, feel its grainy texture in your hands. The texture is similar to granite.

Glass and bubbles

1 Use greaseproof paper to spread the butter over a metal baking tray. Put in the freezer for at least an hour to get cold. Use oven gloves to take the tray from the freezer.

2 Ask an adult to heat about 500g of sugar with a little water in a saucepan. The sugar dissolves in the water, but the water soon evaporates, leaving only sugar.

3 Stir the sugar mixture with a wooden spoon while it is heating. Make sure that the sugar does not burn and turn black. It should be golden brown.

4 Pour the mixture on to the cool baking tray. After 10 minutes, the glassy and brittle toffee will be cool enough to pick up. Like obsidian, toffee cools too rapidly to form crystals.

◄ Holey honeycomb

To make honeycomb, stir in a spoonful of bicarbonate of soda in Step 3, just before you pour the sugar on to the tray. This will make tiny bubbles of gas in your 'magma'.

Layers on layers

Many of the most familiar rocks around us are sedimentary rocks. Particles of rock, shells and bones of sea creatures settle in layers, and then harden into rock over thousands of years. Rock particles form when other rocks are eroded (worn down) by the weather and are carried away by wind, rivers and ice sheets. They become sediments when they are dumped and settle. Sediments may collect in river deltas, lakes and the sea. Large particles make conglomerates (large pebbles cemented together), medium-sized ones make sandstones, and fine particles make clays.

To understand the processes by which sedimentary rocks are made and how they form distinct layers called strata, you can make your own sedimentary rocks. Different strata of rock are laid down by different types of sediment, so the first project involves making strata using various things found in the kitchen. The powerful forces that move parts of the Earth's crust often cause strata to fold, fault or just tilt and you can see this, too. In the second project, you can make a type of sedimentary rock called a conglomerate, in which sand cements pebbles together.

▲ **Cracks in the rockface**
Once formed, sedimentary rocks may be subject to powerful forces caused by the movement of the Earth's crust. Splits in the ground reveal how this strata has folded and cracked.

YOU WILL NEED

large jar, non-hardening modelling material, spoon, flour, kidney beans, brown sugar, rice, lentils (or a similar variety of ingredients of different colours and textures).

Your own strata

I Press one edge of a large jar into a piece of modelling material, so that the jar sits at an angle. Slowly and carefully spoon a layer of flour about 2cm thick into the jar.

2 Carefully add layers of kidney beans, brown sugar, rice, lentils and flour, building them up until they nearly reach the top of the jar. Try to keep the side of the jar clean.

3 Remove the jar from the clay and stand it upright. The differently coloured and textured layers are like a section through a sequence of natural sedimentary rocks.

Making conglomerate rock

1 Put on a pair of rubber gloves. In an old plastic tub, make up some plaster of Paris with water, following the instructions on the packet. Stir with a fork or spoon.

2 Before the plaster starts to harden, mix some small pebbles, sand and earth into the plaster of Paris. Stir the mixture thoroughly to make sure it is all evenly distributed.

3 Leave the mixture for 10 minutes, until the plaster begins to harden, then take a small lump of it in your hand and mould it into a ball shape to look like conglomerate rock.

4 Make some more conglomerate rocks in different sizes with different amounts of pebbles in. Place the rocks on a spare piece of paper so that they can harden and dry out completely.

▲ Natural cement

Conglomerates in nature can be found in areas that were once underwater. Small pebbles and shells become rounded and cemented together by the water.

◄ Clues in the cutaway

The 1.6km deep Grand Canyon, in Arizona, USA, was cut by the Colorado river. The cliff face reveals colourful strata (layers of rock). The strata at the bottom are more than 2,000 million years old. Those at the top are about 60 million years old. Each layer is a different type of rock, suggesting that conditions in this region changed many times in the past. For this reason, sedimentary rock strata can provide valuable clues about the distant history of the Earth.

What's a fossil?

The remains of some plants and animals that died long ago can be seen in rock as fossils. After an animal dies, it may become buried in sediments – rock particles ground down by wind and water. Slowly, over thousands of years, the sediments compact together to form sedimentary rock. The shape or outline of the plant or animal is preserved.

The study of fossils, called palaeontology, tells us much about how life evolved, both in the sea and on the land. Fossils give clues to the type of environment in which an organism lived and can also help to date rocks.

These projects will help you to understand how two types of fossil came to exist. One type forms when sediment settles around a dead animal or plant. It hardens to rock and the plant or animal rots away. This space in the rock is an outline of the dead animal or plant. This is usually how the soft parts of an animal, or a delicate leaf, are preserved. You can make this kind of fossil using a shell. In this case the shell does not decay – you simply remove it from the plaster.

The second project shows you another kind of fossil. Here, the skeleton of a decaying animal is filled with minerals. The minerals gradually become rock. This gives a solid fossil that is a copy of the original body part.

fern

ammonite

▲ Turned to stone

Two common fossils are shown here. Fossils of sea creatures are often found, because their bodies cannot decay completely underwater. Ammonites were hard-shelled sea creatures that lived between 60 million and 400 million years ago. Fern-like fossils are often found in coal.

YOU WILL NEED

Fossil imprint: safety glasses, plastic tub, plaster of Paris, water, fork, strip of paper, paper clip, non-hardening modelling material, shell, wooden board, hammer, chisel.

Solid fossil: spare paper, rolling pin, modelling material, shell, petroleum jelly, paper clip, strip of paper, glass jar, plaster of Paris, water, fork.

How fossils are formed

An animal or plant dies. Its body falls on to the sand at the bottom of the ocean or into mud on land. If it is buried quickly, then the body is protected from being eaten.

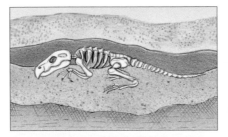

The soft parts of the body rot away, but the bones and teeth remain. After a long time the hard parts are replaced by minerals – usually calcite but sometimes pyrite or quartz.

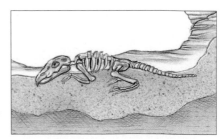

After millions of years the rocks in which the fossils formed are eroded and exposed again. Some fossils look as fresh now as the day when the plant or animal was first buried.

Fossil imprint

1 In a plastic tub, mix up the plaster of Paris with some water. Follow the instructions on the packet. Make sure the mixture is fairly firm and not too runny.

2 Make a collar out of a strip of paper fixed with a paper clip. Use modelling material to make a base to fit under the collar. Press the shell into the clay. Surround the shell with plaster.

3 Leave your plaster rock to dry for at least half an hour. Crack open the rock and remove the shell. You will then see the imprint left behind after the shell has gone.

Solid fossil

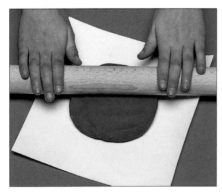

1 Put a spare piece of paper down on your work surface to protect it. Using the rolling pin, roll out some modelling material into a flat circle, roughly 2cm thick.

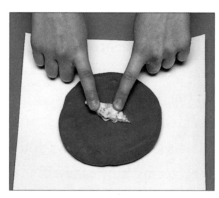

2 Press your shell, or another object with a distinctive shape, deep into the clay to leave a clear impression. Do not press it all the way to the paper at the bottom.

3 Remove the shell and lightly rub some petroleum jelly over the clay circle, which is now the shell mould. This will help you to remove the plaster fossil later.

4 Use the paper clip to fix the paper strip into a collar for the mould. Mix up some plaster of Paris according to the instructions, pour it in and leave it to set for half an hour.

5 Remove the solid plaster from the mould. In order not to damage them, palaeontologists have to remove fossilized bones or teeth from rock or earth very carefully.

These are the finished results of the two projects. Real fossils are imprints of organisms that lived millions of years ago.

Hard as nails!

The best way to learn about rocks is to look closely at as many different types as you can find. Look at pebbles on the beach and the stones in your garden. You will find that they are not all the same. Collect specimens of different pebbles and compare them. Give each stone an identification number and record where you found it, and its characteristics. A hand lens will help you see more details than can be seen with the naked eye. Look for different colours, shapes and hardness. Ask an adult to take you to a geological museum to compare your stone with the specimens there.

You can try simple versions of tests that geologists use, on the following pages. They will help you identify some samples that you have collected. The first test involves rubbing a rock on to the back of a tile to leave a streak mark. The colour of the streak can give a clue to what minerals are present in the rock. The second test shows you how to discover a rock's hardness by seeing how easily a mineral scratches. Hardness is measured on a scale devised in 1822 by Friedrich Mohs. He made a list of ten common minerals called Mohs' scale, which runs from 1 (the softest) to 10 (the hardest). The hardest natural mineral is diamond, with a hardness of 10. It will scratch all other minerals.

▲ Be a detective
Clean a rock with a stiff brush and water. Stand in plenty of light and experiment to find the correct distance to see the rock's details clearly with a hand lens.

beach pebbles

▲ Wearing away
Look at the different sizes of pebbles on a beach. The constant to-and-fro of the waves grinds the pebbles smaller and smaller. Eventually these particles will form sedimentary rock.

◀ Hidden inside
When mineral-rich water fills a crack or cavity in a rock, veins and geodes form. A geode is a rounded rock with a hollow centre lined with crystals. The beautiful crystal lining is revealed when it is split open. Geodes are highly prized by mineral collectors.

outside of geode

inside of geode

quartz

copper

▲ What is a mineral?
All rocks are made up of one or more minerals. Minerals, such as copper and quartz, are natural, solid, non-living substances. Each mineral has definite characteristics such as shape and colour, that distinguish it from other minerals.

Streak test

YOU WILL NEED

Streak test: white tile, several samples of different rocks or minerals, field guide.

Testing for hardness: several rock samples, bowl of water, nail brush, coin, glass jar, steel file, sandpaper.

1 Place a tile face down, so that the rough side is facing upwards. Choose one of your samples and rub it against the tile. You should see a streak of colour appear on the tile.

2 Make streaks using the other samples and compare the colours. Rocks made of several minerals may leave several coloured streaks. Try to identify them in your field guide.

Testing for hardness

1 Clean some rock samples with water using a nail brush. Scratch the rocks together. On the Mohs' scale, a mineral is harder than any minerals it can make scratches on.

2 A fingernail has a hardness of just over 2. Scratch each rock with a fingernail – if it scratches the rock, the minerals out of which the rock is made have a hardness of 2 or less.

3 Put aside those rocks scratched by a fingernail. Scratch those remaining with a coin. A coin has a hardness of about 3, so minerals it scratches are less than 3.

4 Now scratch the remaining rocks on a glass jar. If any of the rocks make a scratch on the jar, then the minerals they contain must be harder than glass.

5 Put aside any rocks that will not scratch the glass. They are less hard than glass, which measures somewhere between 5 and 6. Try scratching the remainder of the rocks with a steel file (hardness 7) and finally with a sheet of sandpaper (hardness 8).

Glossary

A

air pressure The force with which air presses on things. Changes in air pressure make air move and cause different weather conditions.

alloy A material, usually metal such as bronze or brass, that is made from a mixture of other materials.

altitude The height of land above sea level.

artificial Describes something that is not created as part of a natural process or with naturally occurring materials.

atmosphere The layer of air that surrounds a planet and is held to it by the planet's gravity.

atom The smallest part of an element that can exist. It is made up of smaller particles including electrons, neutrons and protons.

B

bacteria Simple living organisms, usually consisting of single cells. Many bacteria are parasites and cause disease.

C

carbon dioxide A colourless, odourless gas containing the elements carbon and oxygen, which is a part of air.

chemical A substance used by scientists, in industry or at home.

climate The typical weather pattern of an area.

condensation The process by which gases such as water vapour become liquids.

conductor A material through which heat or electricity can travel.

conglomerates Large pebbles that are cemented together naturally when sediment collects in deltas.

continental drift The movement of continents slowly around the world.

continental shelf The zone of shallow water in the oceans around the edge of continents.

convection The rising of hot air or fluid, caused by the fact that it is lighter than its surroundings.

counterweight A weight that balances another weight.

crystal A mineral or other substance that forms in a regular, 3-dimensional shape.

D

delta An area of silt, sand, gravel or clay formed when sediment is deposited by a river as it flows into the sea.

density A measure of how tightly or loosely the matter in a substance is packed together.

deposition The laying down of material that has been eroded from the Earth's crust and carried by rivers, sea and ice.

E

Earth's crust The outermost, solid rock layer of the planet Earth.

environment The external conditions in which people, animals and plants live on Earth.

epicentre The region on the Earth's surface that lies directly above the focus of an earthquake.

Equator The imaginary circle around the middle of the Earth between the Northern and Southern Hemispheres.

erosion The gradual wearing away of the land by agents of erosion such as ice, rain, wind and water.

evaporation The process by which something turns from liquid to a gas or vapour.

F

fault A break in the Earth's crust that causes one block of rock to slip against an adjacent one.

fossil The remains of a creature that lived in the past, usually found preserved in rock.

fumarole An opening in the ground in volcanic regions, where steam and gases can escape.

G

geology The scientific study of the origins and structure of a planet and its rocks.

geothermal energy The energy created by the heat of the rocks under the Earth's surface.

geyser A fountain of steam and water that spurts out of a vent in the ground in volcanic regions.

gravity The pulling force that exists between large masses.

H

hemispheres The top and bottom halves of the Earth, divided by the Equator and known as the Northern and Southern Hemispheres.

hot spot A place where plumes of molten rock in the Earth's mantle burn through the Earth's crust to create isolated areas of volcanic activity.

hot springs Water that has been heated underground and bubbles to the surface in volcanic regions.

humidity The amount of water, or moisture, in the air.

hygrometer An instrument for measuring humidity.

I

igneous rock A rock that forms when magma (hot, molten rock) cools and becomes solid. Igneous rock is one of three main types of rock. It is created as hot molten rock from the Earth's interior cools and solidifies.

L

lava Hot, molten rock emerging through volcanoes. Lava is also called magma when it is under the Earth's surface.

lithosphere The rigid outer shell of the Earth, including the crust, and rigid upper part of the mantle.

M

magma Molten rock in the Earth's interior. Magma is called lava when it emerges on the Earth's surface.

mantle The very deep layer of rock that is found underneath the Earth's crust.

metamorphic rock Rock that has been chemically changed by heat or pressure to form a different rock.

meteorologist A person who studies the science and patterns of weather and climate.

mineral A naturally occurring substance found in rocks.

molten Something solid that has been melted, such as lava, which is molten rock.

P

palaeontology The study of fossils.

Pangaea The giant continent that existed before continental drift split the land into separate continents.

precipitation Any form of water that comes out of the air and falls to the ground, such as rain, hail, sleet or snow.

S

sediment Solid particles of rock or other material.

sedimentary rock A rock made up of mineral particles that have been carried by wind or running water to accumulate in layers. Sedimentary rock is most commonly found on the beds of lakes or in large bodies of water, such as seas and oceans.

seismology The study of earthquakes.

Solar system The family of planets, moons and other bodies that orbit (revolve) around the Sun.

solution A mixture of something solid and a liquid into which it has been completely dissolved.

T

tectonic plates The 20 or so giant slabs of rock that make up the Earth's surface.

tectonics The study of the structures that make up the surface of the Earth.

thermometer An instrument for measuring temperature.

tidal wave A huge ocean wave.

transpiration The process in the water cycle by which plants release water vapour into the air.

tropical A climate that is very hot and humid.

tropics Area close to the Equator, between the Tropic of Cancer and the Tropic of Capricorn.

turbulence Air or water movement that consists of eddies in random directions, with no smooth flow.

W

weather The condition of the atmosphere at any particular time and place.

weather vane The instrument used to determine wind direction.

weathering The breakdown of rock and other materials when exposed to the weather.

Index